The Body at Prayer

AN INTRODUCTION

H. CAFFAREL

London
SPCK

*Biblical quotations marked 'RSV' are from the Revised Standard Version
of the Bible, copyright 1946 and 1952 by the Division of Christian
Education of the National Council of the Churches of Christ in the USA,
and are used by permission. All others are the translators' version.*

*Thanks are due to the following for permission to reproduce copyright
photographs:*
*Clichés Musées Nationaux Paris (p. 39); CIRC, Geneva (p. 15);
M. Th. Cattoir (p. 35).*

*First published in French 1971
as Le corps et la prière
by Les Editions du Feu Nouveau, Paris*

*First published in English 1978
SPCK
Holy Trinity Church
Marylebone Road
London NW1 4DU
Third impression 1982*

Translation © The Society for Promoting Christian Knowledge 1978

The translation is by Bob Burn and Heather Le Dieu

*Printed in Great Britain by
Hart-Talbot Printers Ltd., Saffron Walden*

ISBN 0 281 03615 2

The Body at Prayer

Can it be doubted that the body has a part to play in prayer when one sees countless numbers of Indians standing on the banks of the Ganges at dawn, quite still, with their eyes shut . . . or when one sees crowds of Muslims, prostrate before God?

The best lesson I ever had on silent prayer was when I was eighteen, and saw a priest on his knees with his body upright and his face at peace.

So many Christians, who are aware of a call to this form of prayer, do not realize, when they are distressed by their own inconstancy or harassed by distractions, that they are playing at being angels and overstraining their intellectual and emotional resources. Their bodies grow drowsy or fidgety because they are neglected or despised.

Even the body itself asks to pray; it longs for God: 'My heart and my flesh cry out for the living God' (Ps.84). The evidence for this is conclusive for anyone who has ever tried it out; they have found the body a ready companion in prayer. I know of some who, when the soul is oppressed, happily leave the ultimate responsibility with the body: 'Lord, although I cannot think of you or speak to you, please hear the language of my body bowed before you.'

But how can those who despise the body associate it with prayer? First we must think straight. We must reject dualistic doctrines which regard the body and soul as more or less independent and antagonistic entities: for such doctrines either treat matter as contemptible, if not evil, or see the body merely as a prison from which the soul must escape to return to God; according to the followers of Descartes, man is made by putting a body and a soul together. In fact man is a unity, a spiritual body and an incarnate soul. We should not speak of 'the body which I have' but 'the body which I am'. The body is the outward expression of the person: it is 'me in action', 'me present', 'me expressing myself'.

But thinking straight is not enough, we must act accordingly. We must not treat the body casually, like an old bicycle that we throw down on arrival, nor must we comply with its every whim: it is not a dog to which we throw a bone to get some peace; we must not be enslaved by it.

We must love the body; this is part of the obligation to love ourselves. First we must take care about food, hygiene, rest, sleep, exercise, and sport. How many sins of omission are there in this area which are never confessed! Intelligence, patience, and perseverance are needed to train the body, to correct its faults, and to cultivate its virtues. Better still, we must 'live in our bodies', and recognize the 'union of body and spirit', though the phrase will mean nothing to someone who has not experienced such union. The Christian has a higher ambition still: he is working to acquire a 'spiritual body' (1 Cor.15.44), filled with the Holy Spirit. St Paul told the same Corinthians that 'the body is . . . for the Lord, and the Lord for the body' (1 Cor.6.13 RSV). But is this really so surprising when the Christian is fed with the body of the risen Jesus Christ?

This longish introduction is necessary before discussing the body's involvement in prayer. At the very least, the body must not be allowed to interfere with prayer like a badly-behaved child clamouring for attention. Nor should its weaknesses or tiredness inhibit prayer through the physical or nervous tension so typical of our times. Irregular or shallow breathing often hinders prayer, so the body should be taught to breathe. We do not know how to hold ourselves correctly. If the body is not steady and still, it is difficult for the spirit to be truly at ease: that is why this pamphlet pays so much attention to the posture and steadiness of the body. The postures must also express alertness; some comfortable postures make us drowsy.

Anyone who tries to control his bodily reactions will realize very quickly how his mental activities are controlled too.

We must demand still more, and ensure that the body makes a positive contribution to prayer: that its liveliness, its balance, and its harmony benefit the spirit. The body can inspire relaxation, readiness, openness, and the offering of the spirit to God. We should also realize that the body is full of impulses which, when controlled and channelled, strengthen the spirit and support it in its life of prayer.

The highest function of the body in prayer is to provide a language; this may become apparent at the bedside of a loved one who has lost the use of speech and limbs. Using one's body in every possible way to express the deep things of life is a great art indeed. This is true in the relationship between people; it is no less true in that between man and God. That is why, in this little book, we offer not only postures which help us to remain steady and keep alert, but also postures which correspond to different moods in prayer. It is for each one of us in his private prayer to find out which postures produce the best response.

And now I return to my starting point: it is beautiful when the soul of a man can be seen clearly in his body when he prays; when his posture, his gestures, and his movements express the life, the fervour, the adoration, and the love of his soul. There are times when only dance can express all this.

How desirable it is that man should reach this harmony of body and spirit when praying! But we must be convinced that it is possible and want it and practise it. This little book has been published to help in this respect. We are well aware of its imperfections, and believe that the subject deserves a more substantial treatment.

However, in this area, as in others, we must distinguish between what is primary and what secondary. When we pray, it is the activity of the spirit (the 'heart' in the biblical sense) which comes first. Do not forget the words of the prophet 'These people honour me with their lips, but their heart is far from me' (Isa.29.13). But we must not ignore the part which the body may play in restricting the primary activity of the spirit. Yet it is clear that we can pray and pray well, even when we are sick. The body tortured by suffering participates in prayer in a different way, the way of Christ on the cross.

Whether it is healthy or sick, happy or sad, man's body should act as a monstrance, revealing his spiritual life, and should let God's light shine through. St Paul wrote 'Glorify God in your body' to the Corinthians (1 Cor.6.20 RSV), and to the Romans: 'I beseech you therefore, brethren, by the mercies of God to offer your bodies [the Greek word used does indeed mean 'body'] as a living sacrifice, holy, acceptable to God, which is your spiritual worship' (Rom.12.1).

Henri Caffarel

Let us return to the proper use of our bodies. Allow your body the privilege of providing the first firm step of your ascent. What do you do with your body? Left to itself, it only knows how to sleep or to torment you. Clumsy and untrained, it has, in its naivety, taught you many things. But you never realised that you could avoid being kicked by brother ass by mounting him. He is ready to respond if only he can feel you in the saddle! Yes, our bodies pray.

VICTOR POUCEL

> *Let us lift up our hearts and our hands to God in heaven.*
>
> LAM.3.41

Standing

1. (*figs. a, b, c, d, e*) Although often neglected by Christians, standing is the usual posture for prayer in most religions. Amongst other things, this posture expresses reverence, alertness, and a readiness to hear and obey. The Spirit of God made Ezekiel stand up before he spoke to him: 'The voice said to me: "Son of man, stand upon your feet and I will speak with you." And when he spoke to me, the Spirit entered into me, and set me upon my feet; and I heard him speaking to me. And he said to me: "Son of man, I send you . . ." ' (Ezek.2.1-3).

2. As in every posture for prayer, we must find a steady and relaxed position when standing. To do this we must arrange each part of the body carefully.

3. Whether you are standing for prayer or sitting on a chair, your feet should be flat on the ground. They should be together or slightly apart: find out which suits you best. Your legs and thighs should be relaxed, not taut.

4. The position of the pelvis is the key to a good stable posture. The lumbar vertebrae should be exactly in place, and not bent either forwards or backwards. A slight rocking of the pelvis is sometimes necessary to get this just right. After straightening the

*Every day I call upon thee, O Lord, I spread out
my hands to thee.*

PS.88.9 RSV

*If you set your heart aright, you will stretch out
your palms towards him.*

JOB 11.13

lumbar vertebrae, straighten the thoracic vertebrae one by one.
The back must be upright in its natural curve and not under any
stress.

5. The shoulders should not be raised as if you had shoulder-
pads, but lowered and relaxed. The nape of the neck will be in
position when the cervical vertebrae take their natural place
above the thoracic vertebrae. There are two errors to avoid: praying with the head lowered or alternatively praying with the head
thrown back and the chin forward (*fig. v*). You can find the right
position by gently moving the chin towards the neck. This position
improves your breathing and the circulation to the head, as well
as your stability and relaxation.

6. Different positions of the hands convey different meanings
(see *figs. a, b, c, d, e* and paras. i to x, pp. 14 and 16). Look for
example at page 35, which shows the beautiful gesture of offering
of an African Carmelite.

7. The eyes may focus on a point or a sacred object: an icon, a
crucifix, or the tabernacle, for example; on whatever brings
steadiness to your soul. Shutting your eyes may also help your
recollection.

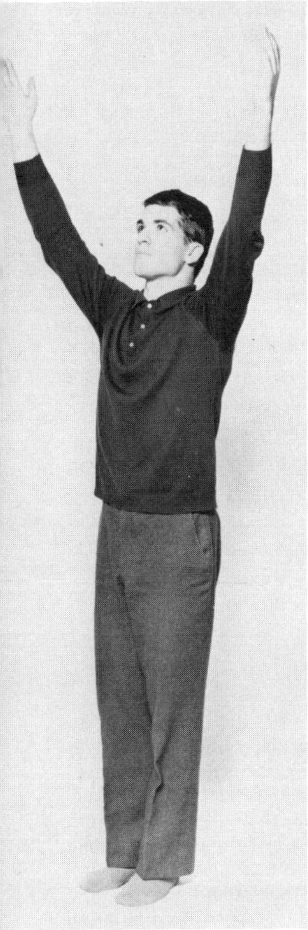

b   *c*

But when you pray, go into a room by yourself, and pray to your Father who is there in the secret place.

MATT.6.6

8. This advice about the pelvis, the back, the shoulders, the neck, and the eyes applies equally whether you are sitting or kneeling and so will not be repeated when we consider these positions.
9. After reading these notes, look carefully at pictures *a, b, c, d,* and *e.* Try to adopt each posture testing the right position of every part of the body by feeling for steadiness and relaxation.

We finally reached a place where we saw my brother standing beside the water with his eyes closed, singing a hymn to the sun. The holy man with me looked at me with his deep brown eyes full of mischief and said: 'I suppose you cannot stay still and meditate on God any more than a tiger can keep to a vegetarian diet.'

DAHN GOPAL MUKERJI

d   *e*

Prayer with the hands

i. Gestures with the hands may be combined with various postures, as we can see in the pictures. Here is a description of the main gestures:

ii. Hands joined: palms and fingers together (*fig. a*). Gesture of adoration and joy, of readiness to respond in the presence of God; particularly suitable when standing.

iii. Hands clasped on the chest (*fig. e*). Gesture of composure which aids recollection.

iv. Hands held out on a level with the heart (*fig. g*). Gesture of asking, receiving, and offering. Illustrated in the photograph on p. 17.

v. Arms crossed over the chest (*fig. d*). Gesture of recollection, of acceptance, and of gratitude, often chosen by painters of the Annunciation.

vi. Hands one above the other in eastern style (*fig. p* and photo of Buddha, p. 39). Hands forming a cradle, resting against the body, left upon right or right upon left. Palms upward, thumbs joined.

vii. Arms alongside the body, slightly outspread, with palms turned towards the front (*fig. f*): gesture of the listening servant.

viii. Gesture of a man praying aloud (*fig. c*): of entreaty, of

testimony, of praise and thanksgiving.

ix. Arms outstretched like the Lord on the cross; our bodies, like the vertical part of the cross, join us to God; our arms, like the horizontal part, to all our brethren. Prayer of intercession.

x. Arms raised and hands stretched upward (*fig. b*). Gesture of pleading. Forceful prayer.

As I live, says the Lord, every knee shall bow
before me, and every tongue give glory to God.
ROM.14.11

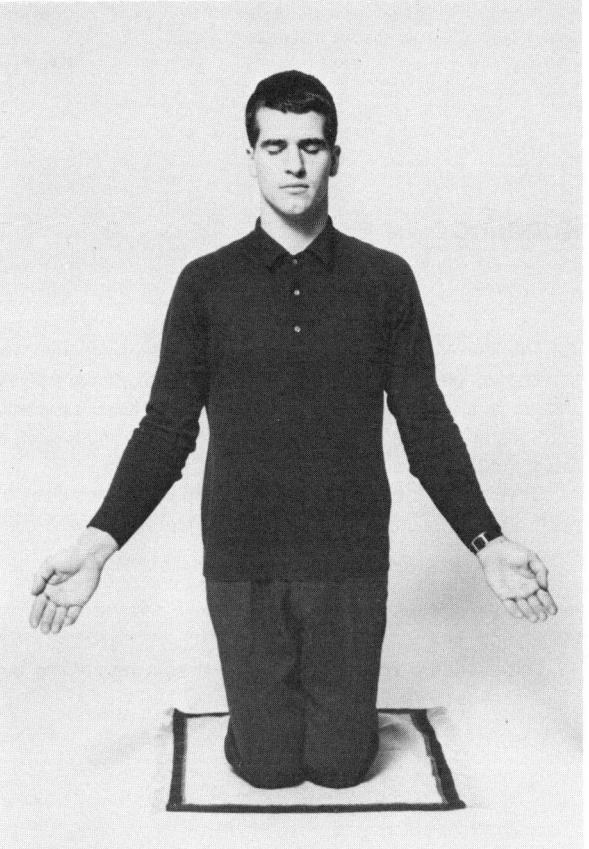

Offer your bodies as a living sacrifice, holy and acceptable to God.

ROM.12.1

Kneeling

10. The kneeling posture (*figs. f* and *g*) expresses dependence, submission, penitence, intercession, and petition. Péguy praised 'the graceful upright kneeling of a free man'. But it is not the only valid posture for prayer as many believe. In the early Church it was even forbidden on Sundays and at Eastertide.

11. Stretch your toes out backwards. Keep your knees close to each other or slightly apart. Place your feet in line with your knees.

12. Your arms and hands may be held in one of the positions indicated in pictures *f* and *g*, or one of those described in paras. i to x on pp. 14 and 16.

13. This posture is a good one when one rises in the morning, but steadiness is more difficult to achieve.

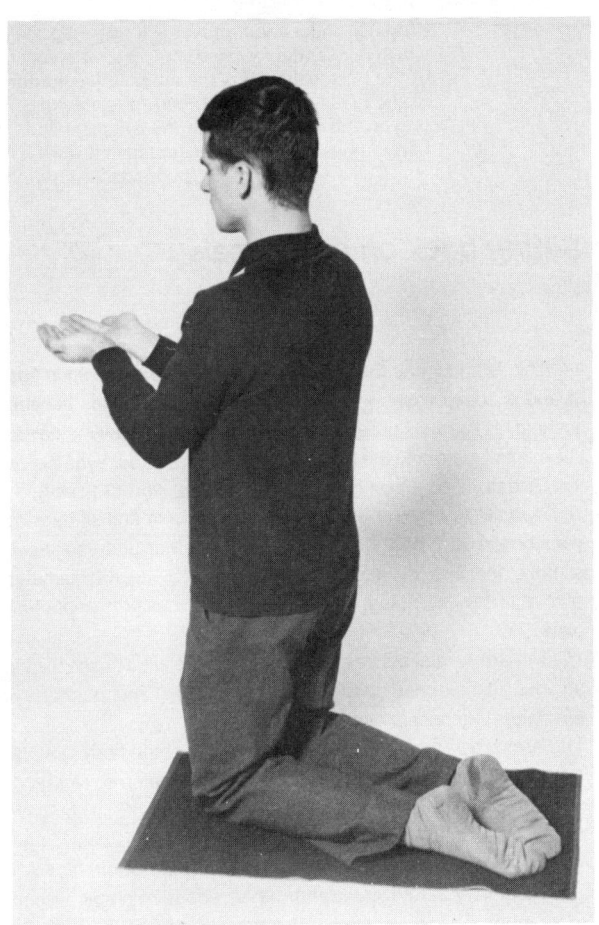

g

> Properly understood, prayer is a mature act
> which is essential for the complete development
> of the personality. It is the ultimate integration
> of the highest faculties of man. It is only in
> prayer that we can achieve the complete and
> harmonious union of body, mind, and spirit.
>
> DR ALEXIS CARREL

Sitting back on one's heels

14. This is known as the Carmelite posture and is shown in *figs. m* and *n.* It expresses expectancy, receptiveness, and attention. 'Behold, as the eyes of servants look to the hand of their master, as the eyes of a maid to the hand of her mistress, so our eyes look to the Lord our God, till he have mercy upon us' (PS.123.2. RSV).

15. In order to take up this posture, kneel down and sit back on your heels. It is best if your toes are together and your heels slightly apart. A cylindrical cushion about 6 cm in diameter, placed under the instep, makes this position easier to adopt (see para. 34).

16. The arms must fall freely, with the hands placed on the thighs, and the palms turned up (*fig. h*) or down (*fig. j*). Other positions of the hands are possible (see paras. ii, iii, v, p. 14).

The arms may also hang freely by the side of the body.

17. If this posture becomes painful (causing cramp or pins-and-needles), change your position slowly (see para. 36). If you have bad circulation in the legs it is better not to use this position.

18. There are more comfortable variations of this posture (*figs. i, j*). They are very stable and permit long periods of prayer without movement. The suggestions of paras. 15 and 16 apply to the

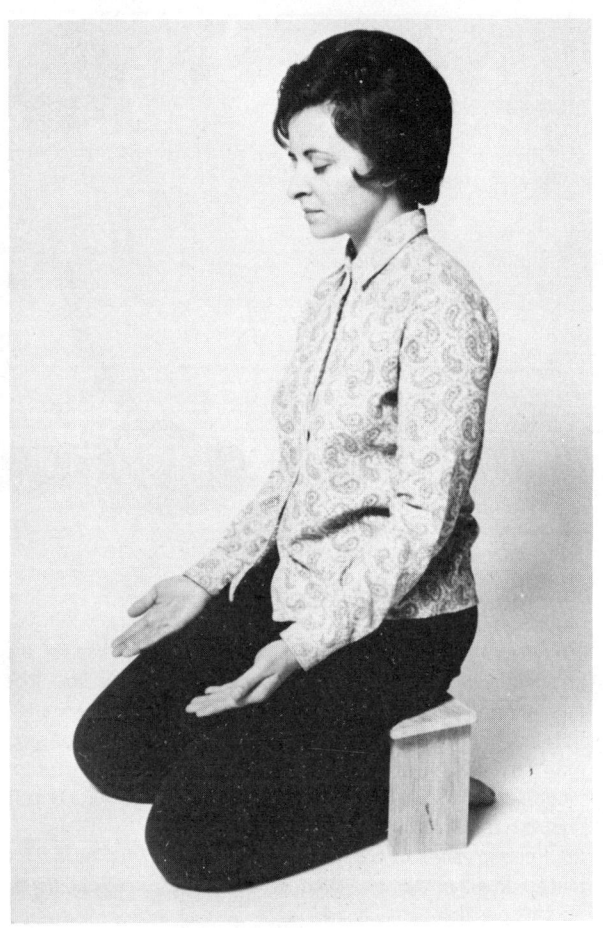

h

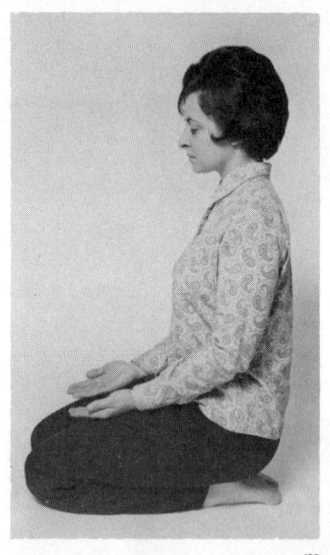 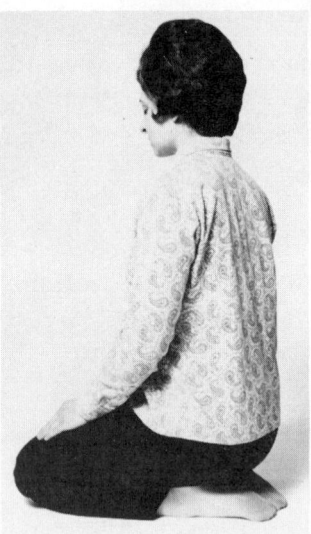

m   *n*

variations, except for slight adaptations required by the use of the stool or cube.

19. First variation: with a prayer stool (*figs. h, i, k*). Once you are kneeling, you place the stool across your calves, with your toes together and your heels slightly apart. Many Carmelites use this position, and it is specially recommended. The height of the stool may vary slightly according to the size of the user: however the difference in height between the front and the back of the stool should not be more than 1·5 cm.

20. Second variation: with a wooden cube (*figs. j, l*). The feet are placed on either side of a cube, or rather a parallelepiped (*fig. j*): note its position here.

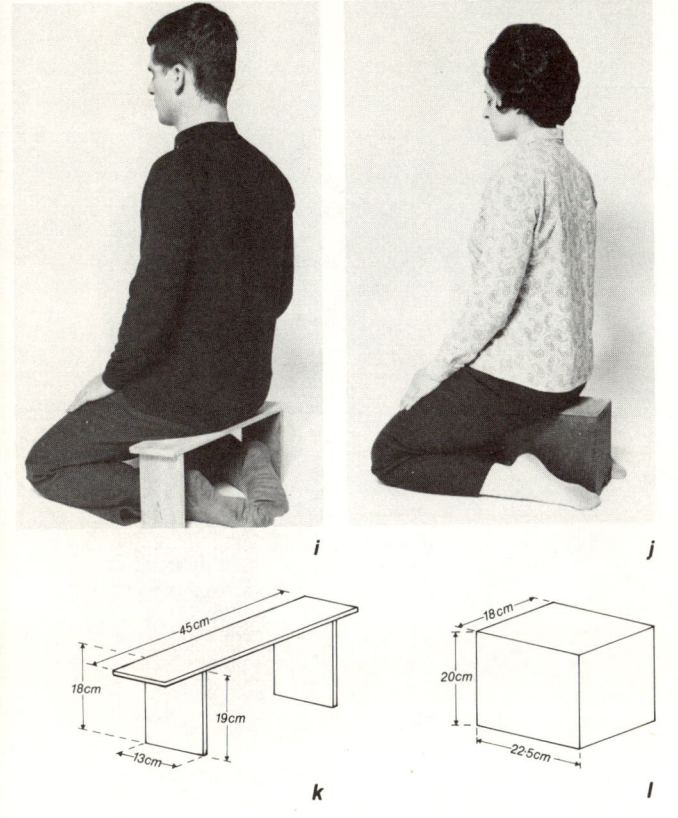

i

j

k

l

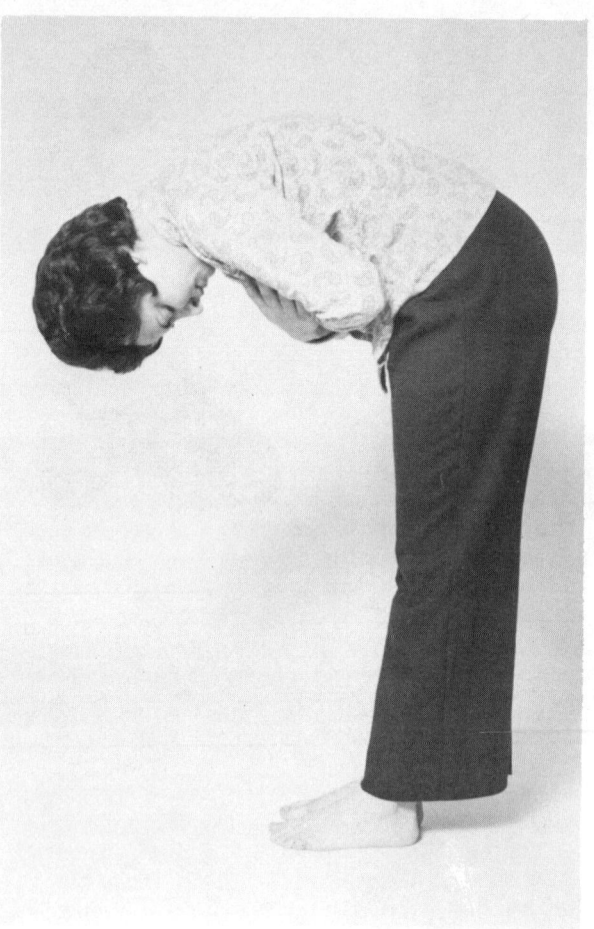

o

Sitting in the eastern position

21. This posture (*fig. r*) has the same meaning as the Carmelite position. It is particularly satisfactory when, having practised it, one can take up the posture without discomfort. One is then, according to the eastern analogy, 'as still as the flame of a lamp sheltered from the wind'.

22. To adopt this position, sit on the floor with your legs stretched out in front of you. Draw up one foot, bringing your heel as close as possible to the body (but do not sit on your foot). Bring the other foot up in front of the first with the heel resting on the floor. As far as possible the soles of your feet should be turned upwards. It is important that your knees touch the ground. Some find it helpful to sit on the edge of a hard cushion of the desired height (see para. 34). (For the position of the hands, see *figs. p* and *q*—a gesture familiar in the East with hands placed on the knees, palms facing upwards, and thumb and index finger together—see also *fig. r* and para. vi as well as the fine photo of the Buddha, p. 39).

23. Placing one foot on the calf of the other leg produces a variation of this position (*fig. q*).

24. If you maintain this position for a long time, it is advisable, in

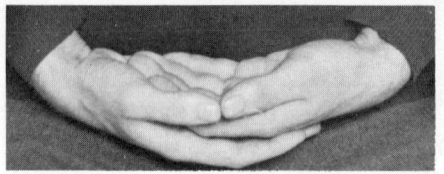

p

order to keep your muscles relaxed and evenly balanced, to place your right leg in front of the left, and then the other way round, the right foot on the left calf and vice-versa. However, some people are only comfortable in one of these two positions. (See para. 36 on how to leave this position.)

There is no need to make any effort: on the contrary, we are offered relaxation and relief. The spirit has needs just as pressing as those of the body. This relaxation is not a luxury reserved for an élite. The spirit needs to pray just as we need to eat, to breathe, and to sleep.

PAUL CLAUDEL

q   r

Bowing and prostrating

25. Bowing (*fig. o*) with arms crossed over the chest or hands placed above the knees expresses humility, reverence, and repentance. 'And Ezra blessed the Lord, the great God; and all the people answered, "Amen, amen," lifting up their hands; and they bowed their heads and worshipped the Lord with their faces to the ground' (Neh.8.6 RSV).

26. Prostration (*fig. t*) is a deeper expression of the attitudes shown by bowing. It expresses worship and adoration. 'When all the children of Israel saw the fire come down and the glory of the Lord upon the temple, they bowed down with their faces to the earth on the pavement, and worshipped and gave thanks to the Lord, saying, "For he is good, for his steadfast love endures for ever" ' (2 Chron.7.3 RSV).

27. Kneel down, stretch out your feet, sit on your heels, and then bow down until your forehead touches the ground, while you remain sitting on your heels as far as possible. Muslims do not sit back on their heels (*fig. s*). Place your hands flat on the ground, putting them on either side of your head (*fig. t*), or fold them under your forehead, or put one flat on top of the other with your forehead resting on them. Breathe slowly and regularly in order to be

Since he is your Lord, bow to him.
PS.45.11b

s

comfortable in this position. At the end of the prayer, do not raise your head and back too hurriedly but unroll your vertebrae slowly from the base of the spine (see para. 36).

28. The 'folded leaf' posture (*fig. u*) is more relaxed: the shoulders are lowered and limp, the arms fall alongside the body, with the palms facing upwards.

Prostration at full length, face downwards on the ground, is sometimes used in the liturgy to acknowledge the greatness of God and the weakness of man as he begs for God's help. It can also meet a particular spiritual need when used privately.

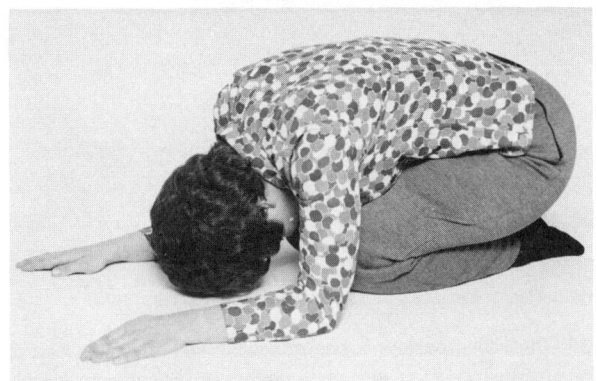

t

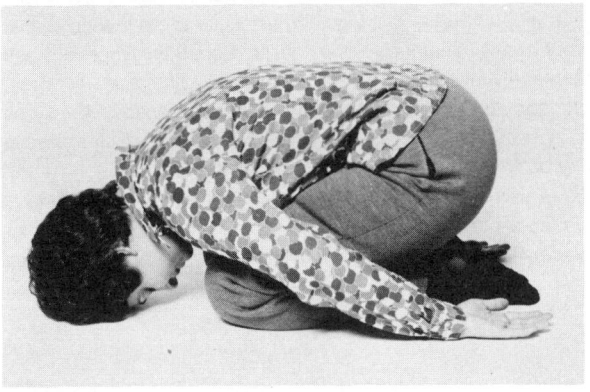

u

Sitting on a seat

29. The sitting posture is one of petition and readiness, and of resting in God (*fig. v*: incorrect position; *fig. w*: correct position).
30. The feet are parallel with the soles placed firmly on the ground, but without pressure. The knees may be slightly apart and the lower leg and thighs should be at right-angles. Never have your knees higher than your hips. If the seat is too low, sit on a fairly hard cushion; if it is too high, put something under your feet (*fig. w*). Keep your legs perpendicular to the ground so that your joints are naturally in the right position. Sometimes you need to move your feet just a few centimetres to find a steadier pose.
31. The arms drop down and the hands are placed on the thighs with the palms facing up or down; or the hands are folded close to the body (see *fig. e*) or make some other gesture.
32. The incorrect position (*fig. v*) shows what to avoid: cervical vertebrae bent forward or back; a rounded back (with lumbar vertebrae bent); lower leg and thigh not at right-angles; arms taut.

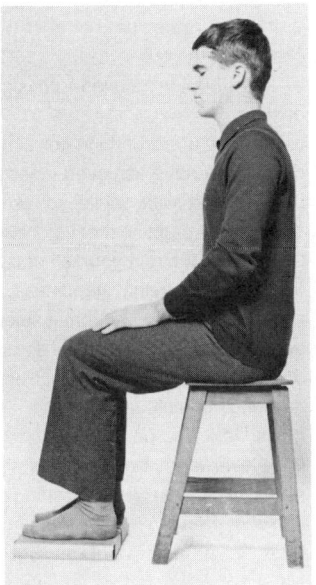

V   W

God knows how to give prayer such an appeal
that you give yourself to it as if you were dancing;
and he also knows how to give it such an appeal
that you take it up as if you were fighting.

ST NICHOLAS DE FLUE

General remarks

33. When you adopt a position, make sure:

a. that your posture is correct (when possible, ask someone to check it with you);

b. that you are relaxed—physically and mentally (see appendix B);

c. that you are breathing correctly (see appendix A);

d. that you have achieved inner stillness.

34. To start with, while you are becoming more supple, you should only practise most of these postures for a short time. You should never strain yourself or maintain a posture for too long. A feeling of well-being, steadiness, and relaxation are signs that the posture is correct and that it suits you. If after several attempts a posture causes discomfort, do not use it.

35. The body's posture must be in accord with one of the corresponding attitudes of mind. The inner attitude sustains and gives life to the physical posture.

36. Never abandon a posture suddenly. Begin by rubbing your hands as if you were washing them, opening your eyes, and blinking; then move your feet and stretch out your legs. You may take up a transitional posture (for example, when you are prostrate, kneel before you stand up).

Appendix A: Breathing

Many people breathe badly so that their lungs are never fully ventilated. They only fill a small proportion of the seventy million alveoli in their lungs with each breath. Their physical and psychological well-being is lessened by this, and consequently their praying is affected too. It is impossible to teach even the elements of the art of breathing in a few lines. We shall simply stress the value of taking a few full breaths before prayer.

Open your window if this is possible. In order to fill a receptacle you must empty it first, so begin by breathing out deeply before breathing in. Breathe out through your nostrils, slowly and silently, from the bottom of your lungs. If you put your hands at the base of your rib-cage you will find that your stomach hollows out and the lower ribs contract.

Keep your lungs empty, without straining, for one or two seconds. Then breathe in, or, rather, let the breath in of its own accord—as a sponge swells up after being squeezed—your stomach swells, the ribs separate, the top of the thorax rises slightly. In so far as you have breathed out properly, you will breathe in properly—but do not try to breathe in fully. Then breathe out again. Breathing out should normally take twice as long as breathing in.

Take two or three deep breaths like this, making sure that you remain completely relaxed. Then let your breathing return to its normal rhythm: be aware of it without controlling it; then, forget it.

Our spiritual being breathes too: it opens itself to the Breath (the same word as Spirit) of God in order to be given life by him, and it responds to its maker in an act of thanksgiving.

Appendix B: Relaxation

The times in which we live impose a lifestyle on us which makes us the victims of many tensions. Some people suffer from muscular tension and clench their fists or teeth for work that does not require it. Some have nervous tension and rush and bustle about; some are overworked; we are all attacked by bright lights, noise, and advertisements. This results in psychological tension: worry, anxiety . . . For others the result is metaphysical or spiritual tension because they have a need for God which is either unrecognized or over-anxious.

We must first of all beware of these tensions: we must know how to stop, to rest, to enjoy ourselves; we should have a hobby. But we must also practise relaxing. Without attempting to discuss this vast subject in any depth, we shall simply make a few suggestions as to how to relax at the beginning of prayer.

Begin with some deep breathing (Appendix A). Then take up the posture you have chosen: for example, sitting on a seat (see paras. 29—32), but do it in a relaxed manner, without any mental tension.

As far as possible, put any preoccupations, worries, or plans out of your mind. Try to adopt the attitude of a child who comes to sit with his father, knowing that he is loved by him just as he is.

After this attempt at mental and physical relaxation, consciously relax the various groups of muscles in your body. Do this as carefully, but also as passively as possible. Begin by feeling the soles of your feet resting on the floor without pressure. Then work up towards your head, making sure that all your muscles are relaxed—your heels, calves, thighs, pelvis, back, shoulders, hands, arms, neck, jaws, tongue, eyelids, forehead, scalp . . . Let yourself be overwhelmed with a sense of well-being. Discover for yourself a good relationship with your body. And then forget it. If you find it difficult to relax in this way, deliberately tense and then relax each part of your body in turn (your feet, abdomen, fists . . .).

Relaxation is an aid to prayer, but how much more is prayer, the meeting of man with his God, the way to relaxation, confidence, and joy.

O thou who art at home in my heart,
may thy voice echo
in my heart.

O thou who art at home in my heart,
I would come to thee
in my heart.

O thou who art at home in my heart,
may I be one with thee
in my heart.

O thou who art at home in my heart,
receive my offering
in my heart.

O thou who art at home in my heart,
may I lose myself in thee
in my heart.

From a Tamil hymn